CONTENTS

Monk in the Refectory   1

PLUSCARDEN ABBEY

The road to Pluscarden winds south-west across the wooded countryside round Elgin. Six miles are all that separate the busy High Street of the county town from this peaceful valley, but those six miles take us back well over six centuries in time.

The atmosphere of quiet reflection and of work dedicated to the glory of God is the same today as it was in the thirteenth century when an organised community of monks first came to this part of Moray; and under the skilful hands of the present-day brethren Pluscarden Abbey is a living entity that is returning again to something approaching its former splendour after so long a period of pillage and decay.

If we are privileged to visit the Abbey today, we can enjoy not only the beauty of its architecture and its setting but also something of the restful atmosphere of devotion that has so deeply permeated this little corner of Scotland.

Profound the peace of Pluscarden,
As if the pine-green closing hills
Shut in the grace
Of God and all his holy Saints.
The Lauds and Matins of the past,
In that calm place,
Still seem to linger on the air
Half-heard, half-dreamt, so wholly felt
There is no time,
The soul is raised above the now,
Beyond the then. Eternity
Of faith sublime
Outlasts all the moods of fate
And savage treacheries of man,
To rise again
Triumphant from defeated stone,
And draw within its sanctuary
All human pain.

THE PLUSCARDEN STORY

A Royal Valliscaulian Monastery

Pluscarden Abbey as we know it today owes its foundation to Alexander II, King of Scots, in the year 1230. Just before this time he had consolidated his power in Moray by defeating other claimants to the Scottish throne, and so this royal monastery would have been a reminder of his power as well as a good work for the benefit of his soul and those of his kin. At the same time two other sister houses were founded by local Lairds, Beauly in Ross, to the west of Inverness, and Ardchattan in Argyll.

The community of monks that lived in each of these monasteries was one of Valliscaulians, a little-known Benedictine Order that combined the strictness and the spirit of fellowship of the Cistercians with some of the solitude of the Carthusians. Only at these three places was this order represented in the British Isles, indeed it seems certain that these were the only Valliscaulian monasteries outside the area known today as France.

The parent house, the Priory of Vallis Caulium, had been founded just over thirty years earlier, during a period of intense spiritual renewal throughout Western Europe which saw the foundation of vast numbers of austere monasteries. The Europe of this time was united in a common Catholic faith and the use of a common Latin language among the educated classes, and Scotland, although geographically on the edge, was culturally a part of the European mainstream.

St Margaret had first introduced Benedictine monks to Scotland at Dunfermline about the year 1070, and with the impact of this new spiritual movement there were almost fifty new foundations of monks and canons made in this small kingdom in the century and a half after 1100. Pluscarden was founded towards the end of this wave of foundations and the original brethren from France must surely have found an echo of the situation of their mother house, lying in a deeply wooded valley in Burgundy, in their new Scottish monastery, nestling as it does at the foot of a steep and densely forested hill. In fact an old name for the Pluscarden valley, the *Kail Glen,* is nothing more than a translation into Scots of the French *Val des Choux* or the Latin *Vallis Caulium.* Like all Valliscaulian monasteries, Alexander II's Priory was dedicated to the two patrons of the Order, St Mary and St John the Baptist, but it was also known as *Vallis Sancti Andreae,* the Vale of St Andrew, and so the patron saint of Scotland was also enlisted as its protector.

Despite its parental ties with France, however, the history of Pluscarden is very much concerned with Scotland's own affairs. The remoteness of its situation and the slender administrative links with the original foundation meant that the Priory went largely its own way, and in 1345 it was confirmed that the Bishop of Moray, whose seat at Elgin Cathedral had been founded also by Alexander II seven years before Pluscarden, had rights of visitation and oversight. Both before and after this confirmation the Priory buildings had probably suffered by attack. In 1303 the armies of Edward I of England had ravaged the Province of Moray and Pluscarden may have suffered damage. The following year there is a mysterious story of a large store of wool and hides being found at Pluscarden which was said to have belonged to a drowned merchant; they were removed by the English and the Prior was paid for storing them. A silver penny of King Henry III, minted in Canterbury between 1251 and 1272, which was found at Pluscarden in the 1990s may be a relic of the English army. Much more serious than this was the assault led by the Wolf of Badenoch in 1390. This powerful man, Alexander Stewart, son of King Robert II, held the appointment of King's Lieutenant north of the Forth. But his judicial authority was disputed by the Bishop of Moray, and the long-standing quarrel between the two men came to a head in this fateful year of 1390 when the Wolf swept down with his 'wild, wikkid hielandmen' from his Badenoch fastnesses upon the coastal plain of Moray, firing the town of Forres, and the town and Cathedral of Elgin. It therefore seems probable that the Priory of Pluscarden, which was under the Bishop's protection, was burned at the same time. Some claim to see traces in the Abbey buildings of the marks of an early fire.

After this, in 1398, Pluscarden was given a new Prior; his predecessor wrote of him, 'We have elected Alexander of Pluscarden, a monk of this house. He is a man gifted and discreet in spiritual matters and circumspect in temporal affairs, he is a priest and of canonical age, born in wedlock, having knowledge and power to defend and improve the rights and possessions of our Priory, which are now poor and meagre, also to repair the ruins of our Church and monastery'. This is significant not only for describing the state of the buildings, which supports the story of the Wolf's attack, but also for the fact that the Prior was chosen by the brothers, as prescribed in the Rule of St Benedict.

In the next century we find Priors being 'provided' by the Pope or the King, which gave rise to abuses. The last Valliscaulian years show an unedifying picture of upwardly mobile monks, some of other monasteries, taking legal action against each other in order to become Prior. That some of the claimants were Cistercian shows, as at least one of them said in his dealings with Rome, that Valliscaulian and Cistercian life were quite similar; but it was clear that the situation was in need of reform.

UNION WITH URQUHART PRIORY: THE BENEDICTINE YEARS

The next date of significance in the history of Pluscarden is the year 1454. From its foundation until this year the names of fourteen Priors are recorded, the last being Andrew Hagis. There are also records of various grants of land, of mills and of fishings on the Spey, which shows that the Priory was not destitute. By the mid-fifteenth century, however, the Pluscarden community rarely consisted of more than six monks, revenues were said to be depleted and evidence suggests that the buildings were in a poor state. The decision was thus taken in 1454, to seek to unite the house of Pluscarden with Urquhart Priory, five miles east of Elgin, which had been founded a whole century before Pluscarden and at this time had only two monks. Urquhart was an ancient off-shoot of Dunfermline Abbey which, founded by St Margaret with monks from Canterbury, was the first community to follow the Rule of St Benedict in Scotland. The Prior of Urquhart, John Bonally, thus petitioned Pope Nicholas V, listing the reasons why the union was opportune. The Pope was at the time busy calling a Crusade, but he ordered the

Opposite: carved stone corbels, arms, angels, foliage and brackets

6

amalgamation by the Bull, *Ad apicem apostolicae dignitatis.* The administrative result was that Prior Andrew Hagis freely retired with a pension, the Urquhart brethren transferred to Pluscarden and half the Valliscaulian monks left to join the Cistercians at the Abbeys of Kinloss and Deer. Ecclesiastically this date marks the disappearance from Moray of the white habits of the Valliscaulians and their replacement by the black of the old Benedictines of Dunfermline and Urquhart. More than this, we can detect the influence of Dunfermline today in some details in the monastic buildings as they survive, including the arms of its founder St Margaret on a corbel in the cloister (although one could note that at the time of the original foundation King Alexander II was a keen advocate of her canonisation).

After this union of the two houses there were a further seven Benedictine Priors starting with John Bonally. Prior William Boyce (1456-1476) had previously been Sacristan of Dunfermline, in charge of the buildings at a time when there was much restoration and construction. He had been sent up to Pluscarden in 1454 to arrange the take-over and receive the professions of the remaining Valliscaulians, and came north again in 1456 to investigate conditions at Pluscarden. The result of this was that he became Prior and Bonally went to Dunfermline as Sacristan where he lived on until 1478. Boyce, with his building experience, may have been the driving force behind a major reconstruction of the fabric of the Priory which architectural evidence suggests took place in this latter part of the fifteenth century. During this time, in 1461, a history of Scotland called the *Liber Pluscardensis* (Book of Pluscarden) was written at the Priory, although not by one of the monks. Prior Boyce was succeeded by

Priors Thomas Foster and David Boyce, the latter being a monk of Arbroath. Robert Harrower, a monk of Dunfermline, had been elected as Prior by the monks of Pluscarden in 1481, but David Boyce managed to obtain the Priory from the Pope. After Boyce's death, however, Harrower was installed as Prior and from 1487 to 1509 presided over a period of reconstruction and growth which continued until it was rudely ended by the Reformation. Harrower sat in Parliament and in 1506 he welcomed King James IV to Pluscarden when it is recorded that the King gave 'drink-silver to masons working on the Priory'. It is clear that the first half-century of the black Benedictines saw much improvement of the Priory buildings. A glimpse of life at Pluscarden is given by a charter of 1508 where Prior Robert granted some salmon-fishings on the Spey to Robert Innes and others as a reward for services to the Priory including 'removing of robbers and poachers' and obtaining from Flanders 'twa tabernacles' for the monastery, 'one at the High Altar and the other at the Lady Altar'. Violence and theft were not uncommon in the Moray of the time, but the people were attentive to spiritual values and concerned for the beauty of the worship of God.

Harrower was succeeded in 1509 by George Learmonth, a cleric of the Diocese of St Andrews and an official of the University of St Andrews: the first non-monk to become Prior. One of the conditions of his appointment was that he become a monk. In 1529 he was named as successor to Bishop Gavin Dunbar of Aberdeen, but he died before the Bishop. The Learmonth arms, carved in stone, have been found at Pluscarden and have been built into the west wall of the Transepts.

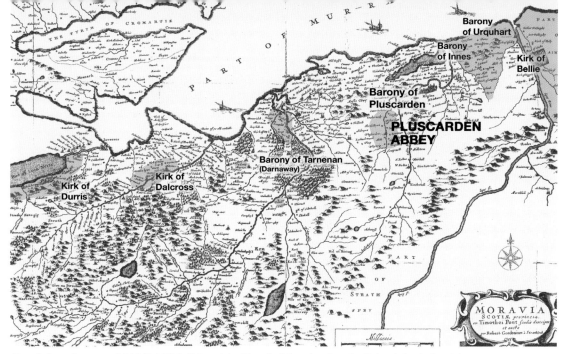

Detail from the map of MORAVIA (Moray) in Blaeu's Atlas, showing the Priory's lands in pink

Dunbars, Setons and the Last Monk

George Learmonth was succeeded by Bishop Gavin's nephew, Alexander Dunbar (1529-1560), another diocesan cleric who took monastic vows. The Dunbars were a powerful and influential local family and already had an interest in Pluscarden: Gavin had attempted to become Prior in 1479 and by 1500 the Dunbars, in the person of Gavin's brother James, had become firmly entrenched as baillies, administering the Priory's lands. Manuscript *Rentals* survive from about this time, listing all the estates owned by the Priory and the rent each paid: part of this was in money and part in produce, barley, chickens, boars etc. The lands were extensive from the Church of Dores on the banks of Loch Ness to farms around Fochabers in the east. Prior Alexander was deeply involved in local society and politics, as shown by his part in the 'bloody Vespers' in Elgin Cathedral. There, on 1st January 1555, a large group of the rival local family of Innes attacked the Prior and his relations who were at their devotions. The Dunbars had not taken off their swords to pray and the ensuing battle led to 'Apostolick *Blows* and *Knocks*', blood being shed and a court case.

This worldly involvement, the detached Prior's House at Pluscarden and the records of legitimation of Alexander's children shows that Scottish monastic life had departed far from the principles of the Rule of St Benedict, but there are no indications of decadence in the community itself which seems to have been flourishing at the time. In the sixty years before the Reformation the number of monks seems to have risen from six to about twelve. In the neighbouring Abbey

George, 5th Lord Seton and his family
by Frans Pourbus the elder
Courtesy of the National Gallery of Scotland

The Catholic religion was prohibited in Scotland by Act of Parliament in August 1560. In September of that year Prior Alexander died, but not before he had anticipated the Reformation by disposing of much monastic property in favour of his family. Tradition has it that Prior Alexander was buried before the High Altar in the middle of the Choir. The next year, however, Mary Queen of Scots ordered the Dunbars to leave and granted Pluscarden to a committed Catholic priest and Provost of the Collegiate Church of Seton, William Cranston, while George, 5th Lord Seton, one of her most loyal servants, was made *Yconomus*, i.e. Steward or administrator of its estates. Prior Cranston died soon after and in 1565 the Priory was given to Seton's son, and Mary's godson, Alexander, who was later sent to the Jesuits in Rome to continue his education. Pluscarden after the Reformation was thus closely associated with the cause of Queen Mary and the Catholic religion. The Setons' Catholicism caused James Douglas to be intruded in 1577, but with the downfall of his father, the Regent Morton, in 1581, the Priory reverted to Alexander Seton. He is often styled 'Commendator', a layman who had the title of a religious Superior and the possession of the house but who did not become a monk or a priest.

In Scotland, unlike England, there was no state-sponsored 'dissolution of the monasteries' at the time of the Reformation, but in 1587 Pluscarden was officially dissolved as a monastery and erected into a temporal Lordship, although the owners retained the title of Prior. That this title continued to be valid in Scots law means that there is an institutional continuity between the current community at Pluscarden and the pre-Reformation monks.

of Kinloss a similar Superior of worldly influence, Abbot Robert Reid, presided over a growing community which was a model of monastic observance and was involved in the best traditions of Renaissance scholarship.

Prior Alexander added to the buildings at Pluscarden by constructing the Dunbar Vestry, and may have been responsible for the fine stone Sacrament House on the north wall of the Choir. A document from 1561, although written just after the Reformation, gives an insight into the life of the community. As well as the monks, there were a Chamberlain, who was a Dunbar, and his two servants, a master cook, a master baker, a porter to look after the gate, and a gardener. It records that £40 was given each year in alms 'to the puir folkis and puir tennentis', and also that 84 bushels of grain were put aside 'for makinge of the malt'.

George, 5th Lord Seton
by an unknown artist
Courtesy of the National Gallery of Scotland

HASARD FORDVARD

GEORGE LORD · SETONE

ÆTATIS SVÆ 27

In
In
Ho

11

Seton, who remained a Catholic, went on to become Lord Chancellor and Earl of Dunfermline in 1605, but he sold Pluscarden in 1595 to Kenneth Mackenzie of Kintail, a Privy Councillor of King James VI. All during this time, as was common in Scotland, the remaining monks continued to live at the Priory, and it seems that in 1593 Seton had a Scottish Jesuit priest staying at Pluscarden. Unlike other Scottish monasteries, however, there is no evidence that any of the monks became Protestants. Two monks remained in 1582, and in 1587 Prior Alexander signed a charter with 'Thomas Ross, last of the monks'. At this time Ross was about 62 years old and we do not hear his name again, although in the 1590s the Elgin Kirk Session records reveal two babies being baptised by 'the monk of Pluscarden'. With this monk exercising his ministry and remaining faithful to the Catholic faith, almost forty years after the Reformation Parliament, we come to the end of the first period of Pluscarden as a living monastery.

'What did Thomas Ross make of all the changes, religious and social, that had taken place in Europe since he had been clothed in the Benedictine habit long ago? Did he think that the old religion would return to Scotland? Did he ever have a vision that, one day, monks of his own order would regain possession of Pluscarden? How one wishes that he had kept a diary, and that this volume had been preserved!'
Peter Anson, 1948.

DECAY AND RESTORATION

There now ensues a long period of eclipse in the religious history of Pluscarden. As a lay property it passed through various hands; after Seton sold the lands to Kenneth Mackenzie of Kintail, the estate remained

with the Mackenzies for seventy years. Kenneth's son Colin, second Lord Kintail, revived a previous Pluscarden connection by marrying Lady Margaret Seton, daughter of Prior Alexander Seton, the Earl of Dunfermline. A successor as Laird and Prior, Thomas Mackenzie, was involved in a 'rebellion in the north, called Pluscardie's', which, after a successful attack on Inverness, was put down by the Covenanters. He fades from our history commanding a regiment of Highlanders at the battle of Worcester in 1651. During this time, in September 1631, we find John Russell of Pluscarden accusing a neighbour, Elspeth Watson, of witchcraft. She was found guilty and was forced to repent while dressed in sackcloth and then swear she would 'charm' no more. In the 1660s, after briefly being in the possession of George Sinclair, Earl of Caithness, Pluscarden passed to Major George Bateman. In 1687 he sold the property for £5000 to Brodie of Lethen, who purchased it for his grandson James Grant. When James came of age in 1709 he sold it to William Duff of Dipple, a local Laird, whose family eventually became Earls of Fife and held Pluscarden until 1897.

In the obscurity of these centuries of domestic change we get occasional glimpses of light: in the 1590s Timothy Pont, a son of Robert Pont who was commissioned in 1563 to establish the new religion in Moray, drew a map of the area around Elgin, part of his project of mapping the Kingdom. To the south-east of Elgin he drew a small sketch of 'Pluskarde' Priory, probably from the west showing that the Nave was not standing at this time. This is the earliest image of the

 monastery; for the next picture we have to wait until the second half of the 18th century.

Reproduced by permission of the Trustees of the National Library of Scotland

The ruins of the Priory, 1799

The Sacrament house

In the late 17th century the diary of James Brodie records:

'23rd September 1680: I went to Pluscarden at night, and stayed with John there. We went through that old ruined palace at Pluscarden and did see the vestiges of a great old building and edifice.

30th September 1680: This day, in the morning, I got an account of the death of my worthy, honest friend John Brodie, in Pluscarden, who died suddenly the night before... I went in the evening to visit them at Pluscarden. I found the woman, her carriage most Christian, and she appears to be a pattern of peace and grace, and submission to God's hand and will...'

John Patrick Crichton - Stuart, 3rd Marquess of Bute

He bought the Priory from the Duke of Fife, and his son later gave the Priory to the Benedicine community at Prinknash Abbey in Gloucestershire.

Concerning the 1750s, the Rev S.R. Macphail writes in *The Religious House of Pluscardyn* that, 'It seems generally believed that the last person who frequented Pluscarden Priory for purposes of Roman Catholic worship was a Mrs Gordon of Westerton, who on certain days repaired thither with her servant-girl'.

The buildings gradually fell into ruin and in 1682 it is recorded that James Ogilvie was paid to demolish part of the Priory, after which the stones were used to rebuild St Giles' Kirk in Elgin. Parts of the Priory Church continued to be used as a burial place by local families and a number of their tombstones remain. The Priory buildings stood unmaintained against the weather; roofs collapsed and ivy grew upon the walls, woodwork rotted into mould and rubble accumulated in the church and cloisters where once the monks had walked. By the end of the eighteenth century, with the development of a taste for the medieval and the picturesque, the ruins began to attract interest and they were recorded in a series of engravings and paintings.

At one point in the 18th century former granary buildings near the East Gate, once called the *Auld Ha'*, were used for local worship. In 1821 James, 4th Earl of Fife, an adventurous character who had been a Major General in the Spanish Army, carried out some alterations in the original Calefactory of the Priory to make that apartment suitable as a Church to replace the *Auld Ha'*. When the Minister, the Rev Robert Dunbar, and most of his congregation joined the Free Church at the Disruption of 1843, Lord Fife continued to allow them to use the Priory. He also constructed the present main road through the valley, replacing the one that passed to the north of the Priory at the foot of the hill, built the 'Gothick' lodge at the entrance gates, reforested the hill itself, and put a roof on the East Range of the monastery buildings. About 1900 a visiting monk of Fort Augustus Abbey on Loch Ness wrote of Pluscarden, 'The monks' dormitory, horrible to relate, had been floored and roofed to serve as a tenants' ballroom! Shooting parties took their luncheon in the chapter-house. But thanks to a Catholic proprietor such anomalies have come to an end'.

The 'Catholic proprietor' was the fabulously rich convert to the faith, John Patrick, 3rd Marquess of Bute who had purchased Pluscarden in 1897 from the 6th Earl of Fife, who had been created Duke of Fife in 1889 on his marriage to the Princess Royal. While the Duffs rose in worldly honour, the stage was set for the Priory to regain its lost glory.

Lord Colum, youngest son of the 3rd Marquess of Bute

Soon after becoming lay Prior, Lord Bute arranged for Mass to be said at Pluscarden in the finely-constructed Prior's chapel on the first floor. The celebrant was Dom Sir David Oswald Hunter Blair Bt. O.S.B. of Fort Augustus Abbey and the occasion was commemorated in this watercolour by H.W. Lonsdale.

THE MONKS RETURN

Abbot Wilfred Upson

Lord Bute continued the restoration of the buildings with the help of his architect John Kinross. In an ecumenical gesture untypical of the time, he gave generous assistance to build the Church that still stands in the glen for the Presbyterian congregation which used to meet in the Priory. The Marquess died in 1900, universally mourned as a devout philanthropist and a scholar, and the property passed to his youngest son, Lord Colum Crichton-Stuart. Having sold all the estate apart from 23 acres around the Priory, he attempted to give it to a religious community. None was willing to take on a ruin and in 1943, having decided that if this failed he would give it to the government, he made a last appeal to Dom Wilfred Upson OSB, the Abbot of Prinknash Abbey in Gloucestershire. Abbot Wilfred was a man of vision whose Benedictine community was growing in numbers and he decided to accept the Priory with a view to its complete restoration. He and Lord Colum have an honoured position in the history of Pluscarden as the ecclesiastical and lay founders of the new monastic community. In 1945 the property was handed over and in 1948 the first five monks returned to resume the Benedictine life last lived at Pluscarden by Dom Thomas Ross. The reborn Priory was formally opened on the 8th September 1948 at a Pontifical Mass before a large congregation in the roofless Church. Dom Bede Griffiths OSB, a friend of CS Lewis who was to become Novice Master at Pluscarden, wrote on the day:

'The sun shone in a radiant blue sky in which clouds rode on a gentle breeze and the leaves of the trees flashed back its light as the soft wind stirred them. It was like a miracle, and when one thinks of how many prayers had been offered with this intention, it does not seem too much to say that it was one: nothing else can convey the air of peace and joy and benediction that seemed to hang over the day after the storm of the night before'.

The community which restored Benedictine life at Pluscarden had an unusual history. They had been founded by a medical student in a house on the Isle of Dogs in the East End of London a year before the Marquess of Bute purchased Pluscarden. That student, Aelred Carlyle, who was present at the opening of Pluscarden in 1948, had originally had a dream of restoring Benedictine monastic life in the Church of England. He had remarkable spiritual power and determination and was able to inspire other young men with his ideal. After years of wandering and false starts, including some time on the Isle of Iona, a stable community was formed and they settled on Caldey

The old Abbey at Prinknash

THE FIRST CATHOLIC PROFESSIONS: CALDEY 1914

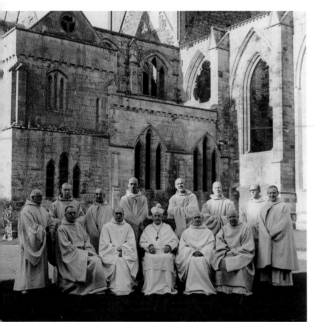

THE FIRST PROFESSIONS: PLUSCARDEN 1950
THE GOLDEN JUBILEE: PLUSCARDEN 1998

Island off the coast of South Wales. A monastery was built and the community grew, but so did doubts about the Church of England which came to a head in 1913 when almost all the community followed Abbot Aelred and Prior Wilfred Upson in deciding to convert to the Catholic Church.

Pope St Pius X and Blessed Abbot Columba Marmion, among others, gave the convert community much help. With the permission of this holy Pope, Aelred Carlyle was ordained in July 1914 and blessed as first Catholic Abbot of the community on 18th October in the same year. With the financial difficulties of the war years and the loss of its Anglican friends, the community was forced to sell Caldey and in 1928 to move to Prinknash, a fine mediaeval house in the Cotswolds which had belonged to the Benedictines of Gloucester. Abbot Aelred's monastic ideal was a strict observance of the Rule of St Benedict in a life centred on the celebration of the liturgy and involving much prayer and manual work. It did not differ much from the lifestyle of the Valliscaulians, and like them the monks of Prinknash and Pluscarden wear white habits instead of the usual Benedictine black.

Six years after the monks returned, the central tower of the church was roofed and the bells of Pluscarden once again rang across the valley. Independence from Prinknash was granted in 1966 and in 1974, after 750 years as a Priory, the monastery was elevated to the status of an Abbey and Dom Alfred Spencer was blessed by Bishop Foylan of Aberdeen as its first Abbot. By the grace of God the community has continued to grow and more of the buildings have been restored with the generous help of the community's many friends. Ian G Lindsay (1906-1966) and William Murray Jack (1921-1999) were the architects during this period. In 1987

Pluscarden adopted St Mary's Monastery, Petersham, Massachusetts, USA as a dependent house and from 1989 the community has helped establish a Benedictine Monastery in Ghana, West Africa. In 1990 a new Retreat House for women, named after St Benedict's sister St Scholastica, was opened, and this was followed in 1994 by the West Wing of the monastery which includes St Benedict's Guest House for male guests. Dom Hugh Gilbert was blessed as second Abbot of Pluscarden in 1992. The Golden Jubilee of the refoundation was celebrated in 1998 and the Scottish composer James MacMillan composed a special piece for the occasion, *Gaudeamus in Loci Pace* (Let us rejoice in the peace of the place), which is a poetic essay upon monastic life at Pluscarden and is designed to match the resources of our new pipe organ. It was later played at Queen Elizabeth II's Golden Jubilee service in 2003 at Westminster Abbey.

The story of Pluscarden is by no means finished. Today we see it as a thriving house, a training-place for Novices, and a place of worship, work and reflection. The physical labour of re-building goes on, and when time and funds permit we shall eventually see a monastery restored to its former glory yet fitted as a religious house of the twenty-first century. Many guests and visitors are received and are able to share the peace of Pluscarden, whose motto, taken from words spoken by the Prophet Haggai at the rebuilding of the Jerusalem Temple in 520 BC, is:

In loco isto dabo pacem,
'In this place I will give peace'.

The monks are chanting
Their office at Pluscarden.
Between here and there
King Macbeth met the witches.
An Orkney earl
Went to meet the Scottish king fearfully.
I think of the monks
With the light of storied glass
On praising mouths.

What more could I ask for?
A little white room
A bed, a chair, a lamp.
I sit at the window
Writing verses on small white
squares of Pluscarden paper.

From *Druim Chinoiseries*
by George Mackay Brown

'Is there any among you who saw this Temple in its former glory?... To work! I am with you, the Lord of Hosts declares, and my Spirit is present among you. Do not be afraid! For the Lord of Hosts says this: A little while now, and I shall shake the heavens and the earth, the sea and the dry land. I shall shake the nations and the treasures of all the nations will flow in, and I shall fill this Temple with glory... The glory of this new Temple will surpass that of the old, says the Lord of Hosts, and in this place I will give peace'

(Haggai 2:3-9)

The Abbey's east front during the Dunbar Vestry restoration   21

Pluscarden in Today's Monastic World

St Benedict

Pluscarden Abbey belongs to the international federation of Benedictine monasteries called the Subiaco Congregation, which includes St Benedict's original monastery at Subiaco in Italy. Pluscarden, the most northerly Benedictine Abbey in the world, is one of fourteen houses of Benedictine monks in Britain: eleven Abbeys and three Priories. In addition there are three Abbeys of Cistercian monks who also follow the Rule of St Benedict, thirteen communities of Benedictine and Cistercian nuns and seven communities of Anglican Benedictines. The total number of monks in 2004 was 458 and of nuns 280. The Pluscarden community consists of 28 monks, some of whom are resident in overseas foundations.

All Benedictine and Cistercian monasteries follow the Rule of St Benedict, written by the Saint in the sixth century. Although called the 'Order of St Benedict', the Benedictines are not really an Order in the same sense as the Jesuits because they are not centralised but rather consist of a number of Congregations, or federations, of independent monasteries. The monastery is the basic unit, the monks belong to their community and do not move about from house to house. The Subiaco Congregation, to which Pluscarden and Prinknash belong, together with Ramsgate and Minster in Kent and Farnborough in Hampshire, was established in 1851 as a reform movement in the ancient Cassinese Congregation; it was originally known as the Cassinese Congregation of the Primitive Observance. The Congregation has an Abbot President, who lives in Rome, and its monasteries are grouped into Provinces according to language or region: Italian, English, French, Flemish, Spanish, German, African, Vietnamese, the Philippines. There are houses on five continents. In Britain there are also monasteries of other Benedictine Congregations such as the English Congregation which includes the Abbeys of Downside and Ampleforth.

The Sacro Speco: St Benedict's original monastery at Subiaco in Italy, which is part of the same Congregation as Pluscarden

The Refectory at
Pluscarden Abbey

THE MONASTIC LIFE

THE LIFE LIVED AT PLUSCARDEN

Monasticism is as old as Christianity and indeed the desire of some men to lead a life of prayer and contemplation withdrawn from general society is a trait found in most religions. The word 'monk' is derived from the Greek *monos* meaning alone, single or solitary, and refers to one who has renounced marriage to live a life of single-minded devotion.

The first Christian 'monks' lived around the Eastern Mediterranean and only gradually did the ideals of monasticism spread to Western Europe, helped by the presence and teaching of St Athanasius of Alexandria. Those who chose to live apart from the world could do so as solitary men-(or hermits, from the Greek *eremos* - desert) or alternatively could join together in communities living the common life (the Greek for common life is *koinos bios* and such monks are known as 'cenobites'). Of necessity, those who live in community should follow a common set of rules, and it was the Rule written by St Benedict that, especially after it was favoured by the Emperor Charlemagne, secured the dominant position in the West.

St Benedict traditionally lived from approximately 480 to 550 A.D. After fleeing the decadence of student life at Rome, he lived as a hermit and then founded monasteries at Subiaco and at Monte Cassino. The latter is now the chief monastery of the Cassinese Congregation. After his death, barbarians destroyed Monte Cassino, as the Allies were to do in 1944, but his Rule survived and because of its discretion and excellence and Benedict's own reputation for sanctity it became more and more popular. Pope St Gregory the Great (c.540-604 AD) wrote in his life of Benedict: 'With all the fame he gained because of his numerous miracles, the holy man was no less outstanding for the wisdom of his teaching. He wrote a Rule for monks that is remarkable for its discretion and its clarity of language. Anyone who wishes to know more about his life and character can discover in his Rule exactly what he was like as an Abbot, for his life could not have differed from his teaching'

Following the Rule of St Benedict the monks' days are occupied with prayer, work and spiritual reading.

An Ordered Christian Life: Prayer and Work

Abbot Aelred Carlyle

'The spirit which we are trying to cultivate is that of assiduous work for our daily bread and the spirit of prayer in the solemn recitation of the Divine Office by night and day'

The way of life of the present community at Pluscarden follows what was established by Abbot Aelred on Caldey and lived at Prinknash Abbey at the time of its foundation: an ordered Christian life of prayer and work, carried on within the enclosure of the monastery according to the pattern established by the Rule of St Benedict. It does not differ in any essentials from the way of life of the original Valliscaulians brought by Alexander II from Burgundy in 1230.

The monks' chief occupation is the love and worship of God: this they try to continue throughout each day and even at night, by being united to God in prayer. It is expressed in the eight choral prayer services and the Holy Mass which they offer in the Abbey church each day; in the love and service which they offer to one another and to the guests received at the monastery; in sacred reading and in their communing with God in the silence of their hearts. Work, often manual work, also has an important place in the monks' life; and the daily timetable, in its typically

Benedictine balance between prayer and work, solitude and community, expresses the monks' priorities. The community provides the essential context for the prayer and work of the monks. St Benedict wrote his Rule for cenobites and so to help build community most days include a period of recreation for fraternal conversation.

A Benedictine Abbey is governed by the monk whom the brothers elect as their Abbot, the father of the community. St Benedict says that the Abbot, 'holds the place of Christ in the monastery'. He is assisted in his responsibilities by a deputy, the Prior; a Council of Deans partly elected by the monks; and the Conventual Chapter, the assembly of all Solemnly Professed monks of the house whose consent must be given to important decisions. Other officials of the monastery include the Cellarer; the Novice Master, who forms newcomers to the monastic life; the Guest Masters; the Infirmarian, who cares for the sick; the Precentor, who is responsible for the chant; the Oblate Master; the Librarian and the Kitchen Master.

The harmony in the community between work and prayer finds its fullest expression each day when the monks worship God together in the choral services in the Abbey church. Here, soul and body are united in the singing of the psalms and sacred texts. Saint Benedict in his Rule calls this the 'Opus Dei', which is Latin for 'Work of God': it is also known by us today as the Divine Office.

A typical weekday in the life of a monk

4.30	Rise
4.45	Vigils & Lauds; Lectio divina in the cell
c.6.55	Prime; Pittance (breakfast); Lectio divina in the cell
8.45	Mass and Terce
9.45	Work, and classes for Novices
12.35	Sext & Dinner
2.15	None, followed by work
4.45	Lectio divina in the cell
6.00	Vespers followed by prayer together in the Lady Chapel
7.00	Supper, followed by Recreation
8.05	Compline
8.45	Retire

Schola at Mass

PRAYER

'Let them prefer nothing to the Work of God'
St Benedict

The monk is a man for whom his personal relationship with God is the most important thing in his life. Prayer is the privileged place where he lives this relationship. The timetable of the monastery is arranged to express this priority, giving the monk three to four hours each day in prayer with his brethren, two to three hours for private prayer and reading in the seclusion of his individual cell, as well as about five and a half hours for work.

DIVINE OFFICE: THE WORK OF GOD. Apart from the daily Conventual Mass, there are eight choral services celebrated each day in the Abbey Church. These extend to the different hours of the day the memorial of the mysteries of salvation which is offered us in the Eucharist. They are designed so that the whole course of the day and night is made holy by the praise of God, a work in which the monks join the angels in their service around the heavenly throne.

The monks begin each day with the office of Vigils at 4:45 a.m., going to the Church as soon as they rise from sleep. Usually in the hours of darkness, Vigils expresses the monks' watchfulness and longing for God: the monk is awake and praying while most people in the outside world are asleep. It lasts for about an hour and combines chanting of the psalms with listening to sacred Scripture and the writings of the great Saints of the Church.

Vigils is followed by the office of Lauds, morning praise, which celebrates the coming of the new day just as dawn begins to break. The psalms, hymn and sacred texts are of a joyful mood, the joy of the morning of the Resurrection and the dawn of the new Creation. Here, as in the entire Office, we give voice to the whole of the material Creation which is moving to its perfection in Christ: 'Bless the Lord all you works of the Lord, praise and exalt him for ever' (*Benedicite*: Canticle at Sunday Lauds).

Between Lauds and the evening service, called Vespers, there are four short prayer services called the 'little hours'. These take their names from the Roman hours of the day at which they take place: Prime at the first hour of the day (about 7 a.m.); Terce at the third hour (about 9 a.m.); Sext at the sixth hour (about noon); None at the ninth hour (about 3 p.m.). These short services last about ten minutes each and are interspersed among the other daily activities, to help the monks to keep praying throughout the whole day.

As evening comes, the monks celebrate the office of Vespers which gives thanks for the day that is now passing into night and calls God's blessing upon all our works.

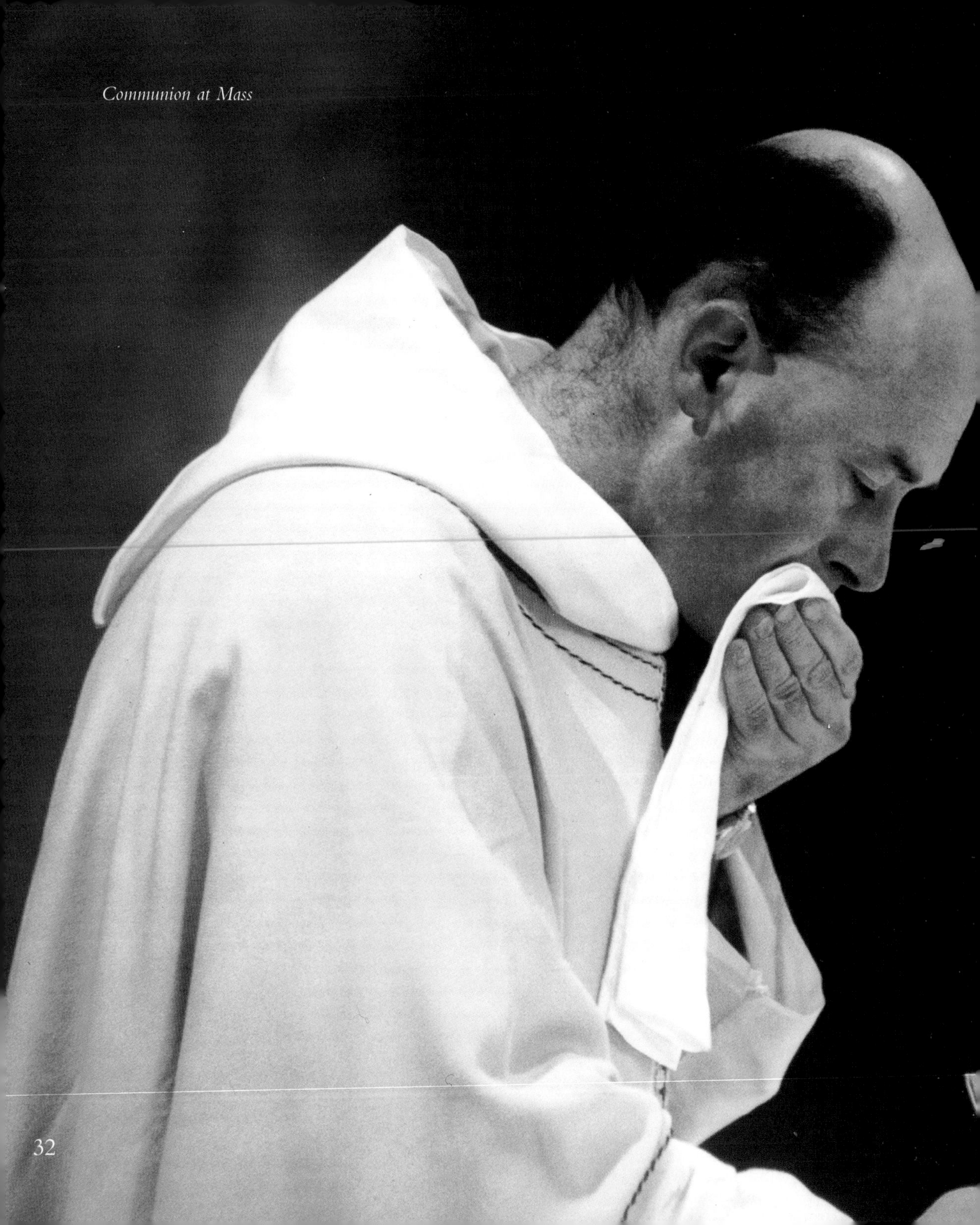

Communion at Mass

When darkness has fallen, the brethren pray the last office of the day, Compline: this completes the daily worship and constitutes their night prayers before retiring to bed, invoking God's protection during the hours of darkness. It ends with an antiphon to the Blessed Virgin Mary, who is the principal patron of Pluscarden, after which the monks and guests are sprinkled with holy water by Father Abbot. They then pause for a while in prayer before the statue of Our Lady of Pluscarden.

For all the liturgical worship at Pluscarden, the use of Gregorian Chant and the Latin language has been retained, and this is found most conducive to an atmosphere of prayer and recollection. It emphasises the objective nature of the liturgy as the prayer of Christ and of his Church, in which we humbly join; it also gives one direct contact with the treasures of Western Liturgy as celebrated by the Saints throughout the ages. Gregorian chant has become very popular with many people who are not Roman Catholic as it perfectly expresses peace and a sense of the transcendent. Although the Church has allowed the use of local languages in the liturgy to aid comprehension, it also teaches that, '*The use of Latin is to be retained*' (Vatican II: *Sacrosanctum Concilium* 36).

Mass: The centre of Each Day

Mass, the Holy Eucharist, is the source and summit of each day's worship. For its celebration, the monks devote the middle of the morning, and it is marked by the use of the most beautiful music and ceremonial. The celebration of Mass is the central liturgical act of every Christian community, making present among us Christ's Paschal Mystery and enabling us to have communion with him by receiving his sacred Body and Blood.

In their daily Mass, the monks find the strength and nourishment they need to persevere and grow in a life of dedication to God's service. They join the angels in the liturgy of the heavenly court and receive a pledge of that coming glory to which their lives are directed. It is significant that the Profession of a monk, in which he dedicates himself to God, takes place during the celebration of Mass: his offering of himself and his consecration are united to the offering of Christ in the Eucharistic Sacrifice.

LECTIO DIVINA. The Rule of St Benedict dedicates certain fixed times each day to spiritual reading (in Latin, *lectio divina*) and this practice is followed today at Pluscarden Abbey. In the Bible God speaks to us and encourages us to respond in prayer: this dialogue is the essential dynamic of lectio divina. Lectio is, however, not just a private activity but part of a great conversation taking place between God and his children throughout history. Lectio divina is a very simple method of prayer: attention to God's Word develops into dialogue and communion. The quiet attentive reading leads naturally to a meditative 'chewing over' of the things read; this leads one to speak to God in prayer and sometimes the Holy Spirit may lead the reader in the paths of contemplation. Such a way of prayer is alien to the information-saturated, results-orientated busyness of the modern world, but it is in perfect accord with the heart of the Christian religion.

As Holy Scripture provides the vast majority of the texts sung in the Divine Office, lectio and Office are but two aspects of the one prayer-life of the monk. This may also be aided by practices such as the Rosary and the Jesus Prayer. At a different level, study, for example reading biblical commentaries or Church history, can help prepare the ground for lectio and the Opus Dei.

WORK

'Idleness is the enemy of the soul and therefore the brothers should be occupied at certain times in manual labour and at certain other hours at lectio divina… for then are they truly monks, when they live by the labour of their hands, as did our Fathers and the Apostles.'

St Benedict

Manual work serves to exercise the body, to furnish a means of support, to foster a spirit of mutual service and to provide opportunities for creativity. The monks' aim is to remain attentive to God even as they work: thus they try to go about their business with a minimum of conversation and a general reverence for silence. At Pluscarden all work is done within the monastic enclosure. The Catholic Church teaches that, '*the principal duty of monks is to present to the divine majesty a service at once humble and noble within the walls of the monastery*' (Vatican II: *Perfectae Caritatis* 9). Pluscarden has no external apostolate such as running schools or parishes, although thousands of guests each year are welcomed at the Abbey. Hospitality is a very important activity for Benedictines and St Benedict, while ensuring that the solitude and separation from the world of the monks is respected, teaches that, '*all guests are to be received as Christ*' (Holy Rule chapter 53). Two brothers have as their main task looking after the guests and another is Oblate Master. Oblates are Christians who are not monks but aim to live according to the spirit of the Rule of St Benedict and have a simple personal rule of prayer. Oblates are attached to individual Abbeys as an extension of the monastic community and our flourishing group is an important part of the Pluscarden family.

Many different types of work are done at the Abbey. Craft work of various kinds has been a tradition of our community since its days on Caldey Island and it has been influenced by friendship with Eric Gill and his circle. One monk of the community raised silkworms and some of the silk produced was used in the coronation robes of Queen Elizabeth II. The stained glass workshop has made windows for many Churches in Scotland and farther afield and monastic sculptors such as Dom Basil Heath Robinson, son of the famous illustrator, have likewise contributed to the beautifying of Churches. Today vestment-making, woodcarving and wood-turning, icon painting and bookbinding are practised at Pluscarden and there is scope for development according to the skills and abilities of those who enter the community. Much important

work is done in the garden which supplies the monastic kitchen as well as providing fruit and plants for sale. Beekeeping is done by the monks, just as it was practised by the brethren here in the Middle Ages. Honey is sold and beeswax is used to make furniture polish and a very popular skin-balm: 'Benet's Balm'. Intellectual work is a traditional activity of Benedictines and the community produces the series 'Pluscarden Pamphlets', which consists of booklets written by the brethren, as well as the quarterly journal, *Pluscarden Benedictines*, which is sent all over the globe. Following in the footsteps of the *Liber Pluscardensis* and the popular autobiography of Dom Bede Griffiths, *The Golden String*, written while he was Novice Master at Pluscarden, the brethren occasionally write books and articles.

In addition to these there are also household tasks and maintenance of the grounds and buildings. These activities are less glamorous but no less important for the community. The brothers need to cook food for over thirty people each day, the cloisters need to be swept, the lawns must be cut, the library of over 30,000 volumes needs to be tended to provide spiritual nourishment for the brethren... There is always work to be done.

There are many jobs and duties to perform at the abbey, including beekeeping, fruit picking and working in the abbey's kitchens

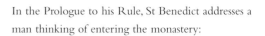

BECOMING A MONK: CONVERSION & THE VOWS

In the Prologue to his Rule, St Benedict addresses a man thinking of entering the monastery:

'Listen carefully, my son, to the teachings of the master and attend to them with the ear of your heart; this is advice from a Father who loves you, freely accept and faithfully fulfil it. The labour of obedience will bring you back to him from whom you strayed by the sloth of disobedience. To you are my words now addressed, then, if you are ready to give up your own will, once and for all, and armed with the strong and noble weapons of obedience to fight for the true King, Christ the Lord'.

All sorts of people respond to this call. At Pluscarden we have had teachers, soldiers, barmen, engineers, students, shipyard workers, accountants and lawyers enter the community. They come from all over Great Britain and even from abroad. All are united by the desire to give up all to follow Christ in the monastic life, spending the rest of their life in the monastery and living under a Rule and an Abbot.

In Baptism every Christian renounces evil. Monks and Nuns are Christians who have received a special call from God, a 'vocation', to dedicate themselves to the service of God without the distractions that come from living in the world. They are required to renounce their own will and also other things which in themselves are good, but which might constitute a hindrance to one wholeheartedly seeking the kingdom of God. Only a great and joyful reward would justify the radical renunciations made by the monk; and only God could provide such a reward.

First among the good things a monk renounces to help him search for God is the possibility of marriage. This is a good and holy state of life in which Christians may live happily and grow in a life with God while bringing new life into the world, but since the very beginning of Christianity, following the example of Christ himself, many Christians have recognised the value of the celibate life as one in which individuals can give themselves wholeheartedly to the love and service of their Lord and their neighbour. The monk also renounces the ownership of private property. All the goods of the monastery are held in common, and a monk may not call anything his own. He has no money, but is supplied with the items which he needs in order to live his daily life. When necessary, he must ask for these from his superiors in the monastery. This fulfils the command of Jesus: '*Whoever of you does not renounce all that he has cannot be my disciple*' (Mk 14:33). The third enunciation the monks make is that of following their own private inclinations. Instead they submit themselves in obedience to the guidance of the Abbot, the spiritual father of the monastery. In committing themselves to obedience the monks imitate Christ, who '*became*

obedient unto death' (Phil 2:8) and said, '*I have come down from heaven, not to do my own will, but the will of him who sent me*' (Jn 6:38).

These three renunciations are consecrated chastity, poverty and obedience. Instead of professing these three vows explicitly, like Franciscans and members of other more recent Orders, the Benedictine takes vows of stability, conversion of life (in Latin, *conversatio morum*) and obedience. This monastic profession includes the vows of chastity, poverty and obedience. *Conversatio morum* means that the monk binds himself to live the monastic life according to the Rule of St Benedict; by ascetic struggle he aims, with the help of the Holy Spirit, to rid himself of worldly attitudes in order to strive towards the perfection of Gospel love.

Stability makes the monk a member of the family of the monastery of his profession. This usually means staying for life in this monastery, but it sometimes happens that a monk may be needed to help in another monastery, especially if a new one is being founded. Closely linked to stability in the community is the practice of enclosure: staying in the monastery and reducing travel to a minimum. This voluntary 'withdrawal into the desert' minimises distractions and gives time and space for prayer.

I have come down from heaven, not to do my own will, but the will of him who sent me

How to Become a Monk :

'Test the Spirits' (1 John 4:1)

Since the renunciations which a monk is required to make are so radical, and the external renunciations are only the beginning and the prelude to a more radical interior renunciation, it is very important that there be an extensive period of trial for those drawn to our life, so that the community and the aspirant can discern whether he is truly called by God. The candidate must be single, male, Catholic and free from any debts or responsibilities. St Benedict wrote that, '*the concern must be whether the novice truly seeks God, and whether he shows eagerness for the Work of God, for obedience and for trials*' (Holy Rule, 58:7).

After visiting the Community and talking with the Novice Master, if it seems the applicant has a genuine vocation he is invited to enter the monastery as a Postulant ('*one who asks*'). About six months postulancy is followed by at least a year's noviciate, which begins with the rite of monastic initiation during which the Novice is given a new name and the tonsure. The noviciate is a period of formation in the monastic life and prayer, with classes in the Holy Rule, Monastic Tradition, the Psalms, Latin and Gregorian Chant, as well as participation in the work of the community. During it the Novice is free to leave at any time and may also be asked to leave. The Postulants and Novices wear a grey habit, over which in winter they wear a black cloak for the choir offices.

After the end of the noviciate, there is a vote of the community to allow the novice to take Temporary Vows and receive the white habit as a sign of consecration. With the white habit the junior monk in Temporary Vows wears a white cloak in Choir, while the monk in Solemn Vows wears the full monastic cowl as a sign of his consecration for life. Temporary Vows are made at Mass and last for a minimum of three years. During this time the junior monk receives further formation in Scripture, Catholic Theology and Liturgy, to help him to live a fruitful monastic life. Then, after another vote of the community, he may proceed to Solemn Vows, which make him a full member of the community. There is therefore ample time, at least four and a half years, to make a free and informed decision to commit himself to the monastic life as it is lived at Pluscarden. The brother can then make his Solemn Vows with a peace of soul founded upon having given himself totally to Christ, who has called him to this life. The ceremony in which a monk professes his final vows and is consecrated is very beautiful and moving: the whole community unites in prayer that God may grant him perseverance and growth in the life of the Spirit. For those who are thus called it is the best way to serve God and the surest way to peace in this life and eternal beatitude in the next. '*He who can receive this, let him receive it*' (Mt 19:12).

WHAT USE IS THE MONASTIC LIFE?

The monastic life is the free response to a divine call of those who desire wholeheartedly to give themselves to a daily loving service of the Lord in community under a Rule and an Abbot. As well as helping the monk along the road that leads to salvation, the monastery is also useful to the Church and to humanity in general: *'How can contemplatives be considered alien to human society if in them humanity achieves its fulfilment?'* (*Venite Seorsum* 3).

The Church has always delighted in the many gifts which the Holy Spirit has manifested in Christians, and has particularly blessed and encouraged those who wish to dedicate themselves wholly to a life of prayer, which embodies the noblest of all human aspirations: total union with God. From the earliest days of the Church, Christians have recognised the value and desirability of having in their midst some of their number who are wholly dedicated to prayer. These, though not participating in the many necessary active works in the world, nonetheless share by desire in this external service of the Lord. They add to its fruitfulness by offering it in prayer to God and making intercession for the particular needs of the Church and the world. A monastic Father once said, *'A monk is one who is separated from all, and united to all'*. One can also see a prophetic witness in the monastic life.

Like the prophets of old who set before their disciples examples of counter-cultural and even bizarre behaviour in order to convey an important message, it sets before today's world a striking lesson on the primary importance of the love and worship of God.

'In present-day society, which so easily rejects God and denies his existence, the life of men and women completely dedicated to the contemplation of eternal truth constitutes an open profession of the reality of both his existence and his presence' (*Venite Seorsum* 5).

The monastery is valuable for all those who come as guests, seeking a place of prayer and peace where they can renew the focus of their lives upon God, and from there return refreshed to their daily lives in the world. It can also provide a spiritual centre for the local Church and a place where the riches of Catholic faith and worship can be shared with those of other traditions.

The brethren of Pluscarden are pleased to have good relations with other Christian Churches and communities, and on a number of occasions have welcomed to the Abbey the Moderator of the General Assembly of the Church of Scotland. Many people of all beliefs can appreciate the dedication of monks and there have been countless testimonies that Pluscarden is indeed a place where God's promise is true: *'In this place I will give peace'*.

A Tour of the Abbey

Days of my childhood in the grey old garden,
Books that engaged my green unknowing mind;
Hours in the haunted cloisters of Pluscarden
How fair you seem, how faint, how far behind.

Andrew Lang
on remembering reading *Jane Eyre* in 1852,
aged 8, in the cloister at Pluscarden.

41

42

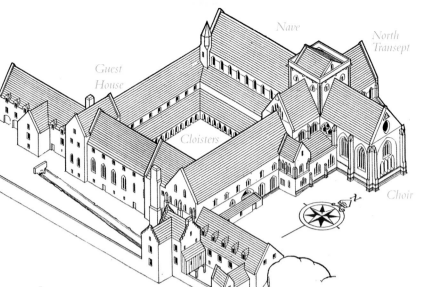

Opposite:
Pre-restoration
Pluscarden Priory,
showing the Tower
and the ruins of the Nave
and South Transept.
Watercolour by
Thomas Girtin 1793.
Courtesy of The Bridgeman Art Library.

PLAN OF THE ABBEY

1 Cloisters
2 Site of Nave
3 Shop and Toilets on site of Nave Aisle
4 Crossing and Tower
5 Sanctuary and Choir
6 Dunbar Vestry
7 North Transept
8 South Transept
9 Transept Aisles
   (Medieval Chapels)
10 Lady Chapel
11 Chapter House
12 Slype (Library)
13 Refectory and Kitchen
   (Medieval Day Room)
14 South-east wing with cellars under
15 Rere-dorter
16 Prior's Lodging
17 Infirmary and cells
   (Medieval Calefactory)
18 Workshops on site of
   Medieval Refectory
19 West Range with
   St Benedict's guest house
20 Probable site of South-west wing:
   Kitchens ?

■ MEDIEVAL BUILDINGS

▨ MEDIEVAL FOUNDATIONS

▨ RECONSTRUCTION
   AND NEW BUILDINGS

43

First Impressions

The old Pilgrim Road to Pluscarden hugged the forested hillside north of the valley and swept round to the imposing North Gate of the Priory precincts. Today, however, the visitor leaves his car at the East Gate and walks up the drive until he suddenly beholds the majestic east gable of the Abbey Church across the lawns. From this approach it is possible to form a clear picture of the composition of the East Range of Pluscarden Abbey, which was clearly designed to make a strong impression on a visitor. Dominating the whole group is the massive block of the central tower and the North and South Transepts of the Church, and – to the east of these – the Choir with its finely composed east window. At either end of the hood moulding around this window are finely carved heads of a King and a Queen: Alexander II and Queen Joan? Above the main group of windows are a large vesica and a trifoliated triangle which admit light to the space below the roof. In the former is a line design of St Benedict holding his Rule. Following the Cistercian ideal of simplicity, the Tower is rather squat and barely rises above the roof-line. It has a characteristically Scottish late-Gothic saddle-back roof. Immediately south of the Choir and South Transept is the lower projection of the Lady Chapel, originally the Sacristy, and above this is the Prior's Chapel with the small lancet of its tiny antechamber to the right of the window behind its altar. Above this is the round window of the former Noviciate Chapel of SS Maurus and Placid.

Beyond this to the south can be seen the long block of the domestic buildings, re-roofed in 1960 to create an extra floor, containing Chapter House, Library and Refectory at ground level and dormitories above. This block forms the east side of the cloister garth.

44

This wing has been completely restored to full use in the daily life of the Abbey. To the left of the East Range may be seen the ruins of the Tower House that was the Prior's Lodging, and to the east of that the remains of the Rere-dorter or monastic toilets under which is a stone channel originally flushed by running water. The Precinct Wall, part of which can be seen as one comes up the drive, is the second largest in length in Scotland, only that of St Andrews being larger. It encloses ten acres. The North Gate was originally protected by a large gatehouse, the ruins of which can still be seen from the hill field. It has a room at ground level which some think was a prison cell, serving the needs of the Court of Regality centred on Pluscarden where the Prior had jurisdiction almost as great as that of the King. In the north precinct wall there still survive the recesses, called bee-boles, in which the monks long-ago kept their wicker beehives, or skeps, from which came wax

for candles and honey to sweeten food and drink. An 1812 water colour by Mr Shanks of Elgin seems to show an ornate but ruined medieval East Gate where the present entrance is.

In the Cemetery behind the hedge are the graves of monks and friends of the monastery and also a fine Calvary in native oak, the work of Marvin Elliott, a gift in memory of Richard Simpkin. All around the Abbey buildings stand magnificent trees, some of them perhaps at only two or three generations remove from the plantings of the first monks of Pluscarden, and, among them, the bird-song that accompanies the visitor as he strolls in the grounds is something that he will not soon forget.

The North Transept

The Nave and Transepts

Walking round to the north of the buildings, the visitor today enters the Church by a finely detailed doorway in the North Transept under an impressive array of windows. To the right as one enters the Transepts is a series of interpretive boards and paintings giving the history of the Monastery and on the wall behind are some ancient tombstones. The oldest of them dates from 1480 and bears the name DOM. GUL. DE BYRNET (Dom William of Birnie). He was clearly a priest to judge from the carved representations of a chalice and missal, but probably not the Prior of that name. One plain stone near the north door is from the tomb of a monk, the lettering around the edge identifies him as 'Dom James Wyatt priest and professed monk who died on the 26th December 1515' (in Latin, *hic iacet dominus Jacobus Viot sacerdos et professus qui obiit xxvi die decembris anno domini MDXV*). The older gravestones have symbols of Christian hope such as the Cross, but the later post-Reformation memorials have bones, coffins and grave-digging implements carved on them. The newly-faced stone wall in the middle of the west wall of the Transepts fills what was originally an open arch into the Nave. A tradition first noted in 1761 says that the Nave was never built: A Catholic priest, Rev John Geddes, visiting Pluscarden then wrote that, "I am in some Doubt whether or not the Western Part of the Church has ever been finished, the Ruines of it being now only three or four feet high whereas the Walls of the other Parts are almost entire and the Inhabitants there have a vulgar tradition that when the Church was all finished excepting that Western Part the builders heard a Voice saying, *'The Monastery of Pluscartie Begun; but ne'er shall ended be'* ......and then desisted"

Architectural evidence, however, suggests that the Nave was indeed built, but one can read this prophecy as predicting the return of the monks to the Vale of St Andrew! One can see the lowest courses of the nave walls around the small lawn outside, with the base of a fine doorway at the west end. Low modern buildings accommodating lavatories and the Abbey Shop mark the line of the South Aisle and of the north side of the cloister square. On the top of the wall can be seen a weather-vane made by Br Patrick Bergin and designed by Br Herbert Kaden showing the Wolf of Badenoch attacking the Priory. Perhaps the Nave will one day be rebuilt?

Standing beneath the central Tower with the North and South Transepts to left and right of us, we can at once appreciate the scale and dignity of the Abbey building and at the same time the sheer physical problems of reconstruction that face the present-day community. It was only in 1961 that, through the generosity of Dr Archie Wallace, the Transepts were roofed. Then came the gift of the stained glass windows in the north wall, in contemporary style, executed by Sadie McLellan of Glasgow. The great Rose Window in the north gable is sixteen feet in diameter and the theme of the glass is taken from the 12th chapter of the Book of Revelation: *The Woman clothed with the Sun.*

The stained glass in the Abbey is described in greater detail below. This north wall of the Transept is in fact a veritable wall of light, and the airiness of its conception has been compared with the masterly window-constructions of Elgin Cathedral and York Minster.

Today the severity of grey stone surrounds us, but in the middle-ages the Priory Church must have blazed with colour from the windows and from the polychrome decorations upon the walls. Traces of 15th century fresco can in fact still be seen around the Chancel Arch which led originally from the Transepts into the Choir. It is perhaps difficult at first to decipher the designs, but on the north soffit the figure of *St John the Evangelist* can be seen writing in a scroll and with his symbolic eagle beside him. In the centre of the arch behind the arms of the cross, less clearly, the Sun, Moon and Stars recall the text of the Rose Window glass, while on the south soffit there may have been represented an Annunciation. It is recorded that the Abbot of Kinloss Abbey just over the hill from the Vale of St Andrew employed a skilled painter, Andrew Bairhum, in 1538 to decorate his Church, and he may also have been employed at Pluscarden. Examples of pre-Reformation fresco of this sort are extremely rare in Scotland. Across the Chancel Arch a light gallery has now been constructed and on it are emblazoned the arms of most of the secular families that owned Pluscarden between 1560 and 1943. In order from left to right they are: 1: Seton; 2: Mackenzie of Kintail; 3: Mackenzie of Tarbat; 4: Sinclair, Earl of Caithness; 5: Grant of Grant; 6: Duff of Braco; 7: Duff, Earl of Fife; 8: Crichton-Stuart, Marquess of Bute. The Rood, or large Crucifix with statues of Our Lady and St John, is early 20th Century Bavarian, carved, it is said, at Oberammergau. It was formerly in the Convent of the Anglican Sisters of the Holy Cross at Haywards Heath.

The Great Rood in the Chancel Arch

48

The Transepts may have been the first part of the Priory constructed in the thirteenth century. The east walls of the North and South Transepts show two different responses to the same architectural problems. Each has two arches at ground level which are now blocked up but would each originally have had wooden screens with doors leading into the chapels beyond. Above these there are different arrangement of clerestory windows incorporating a passageway within the wall; the east wall of the North Transept, although plainer, was probably built later than that in the South. Structural alteration is plainly to be seen in the Chancel Arch which must originally have accommodated a rood-screen, and a small staircase can still be seen leading up to the rood-loft. The fill-in masonry that has reduced the original opening is obviously repair work, probably instituted after the burning of the 1390s, but the remains of an older clustered column survive. If one looks up at the floor of the tower bell-chamber above one can see evidence in each corner that the roof of the Crossing was originally stone-vaulted. There are three bells in the Abbey Tower, all of which were re-cast and consecrated in 1954, and they are dedicated to the three patrons of the Abbey: Our Lady, St John the Baptist and St Andrew. The smallest, St Andrew, was originally a ship's bell, and the other two came here via Caldey from the Anglican Abbey of Llanthony.

On the walls of the Transepts six consecration crosses can be seen, while beside the west door are carved the arms of the penultimate pre-Reformation Prior, George Learmonth; another finely-moulded arch in the west wall was obviously designed to give access to the south aisle of the Nave.

At the south west corner of the South Transept is the night-stair leading to the monks' dormitory. Under it a curious little vaulted chamber has been found with three aumbries or cupboards within its walls. To the east of the stairs, over the St Andrew's Altar is a shrine containing an icon of the Blessed Virgin Mary, Daughter of Zion, painted by a Benedictine nun on the Mount of Olives, Jerusalem. Since being installed in the Jubilee year 2000, it has become a focus of devotion.

THE TRANSEPT AISLES

Passing through a communicating door, the visitor enters the original Transept Chapels, now for the time being combined to form two Chapels for the laity either side of the High Altar. The most distinguished feature of these is the fine groined roof, and one can also see holes in the columns supporting it which would have held wooden beams forming carved partitions separating each Transept Aisle into two Chapels. The east walls of these aisles must originally have formed the reredos behind the altars of the side Chapels, and it is no surprise therefore to find faint survivals of mural decorations here too; at the south-east corner the subject matter can be identified from old photographs as a portrayal of *St John the Baptist*.

At this south end of the Transept Aisles a squint, probably installed during the

The Visitation window

fifteenth century rebuilding, allows a view of the Altar of the Lady Chapel where the Blessed Sacrament is now reserved. The Altar reredos has panels either side of the Tabernacle which both contain censing angels carved in low relief by Alfred James Oakley (1878-1959). The walls of this squint were once covered with fresco and the small columns on either side are worthy of notice for their curious asymmetry, two having plain capitals, another carved with foliage and the fourth with the figures of two angels. The Lady Chapel is not open to the public but contains choir stalls and a small gallery made by the monks. It also has the remains of mediaeval wall-paintings.

Before we leave the aisles we should notice the fine stained glass window on the theme of *The Visitation*, described in greater detail below.

The Altar reredos angels carved by Alfred James Oakley

THE CHOIR

The Choir was re-roofed in 1982 following an appeal launched in 1980 to mark the 750th anniversary of the founding of the Abbey in 1230 and 1,500 years from the birth of St Benedict. The best view for a visitor is through the glass doors below the great Crucifix, looking towards the original site of the High Altar, although one can also see from the two Transept Chapels. The Choir and Sanctuary, the area around the Altar, are sacred places and are thus not open to the public.

The first thing one notes are the fine stained-glass windows in the great East Window which show Christ in glory bearing the bread and wine of the Eucharist, and in the lower lancets, vines and grapes, corn and bread. These were designed and made in the Abbey workshops by Br. Gilbert and are described in more detail later in this book.

The sandstone High Altar stands in the centre of the Sanctuary and was originally in the Blessed Sacrament chapel at Fort Augustus Abbey on Loch Ness. On the closure of that community it  was transported and re-erected at Pluscarden. As Christians from very early days have celebrated Mass on the tombs of the martyrs, it is an ancient custom to insert relics of the Saints into Altars. The Pluscarden Altar is

The Sanctuary

dedicated in honour of St Andrew and St John the Baptist and contains relics of St Andrew and St Innocentia in a small silver box, as well as bones of the early Martyrs Saints, Eutropia of Alexandria, Revocatus and Maximus, a Roman legionary martyred at Ostia. The short antependia on the Altar, in liturgical colours, were woven by one of the brethren. On the north wall of the Sanctuary is the distinctive statue of Our Lady of Pluscarden by Alfred James Oakley. The brethren pray before this statue each evening after Compline.

On the west wall are two large icons of St Andrew and St John the Baptist by Sr Petra Clare which complete the set of images of the three patron saints of the Abbey. It was traditional in the middle ages to have such 'principal images' in the Sanctuary. St Andrew and St John hold scrolls with their own words written in Greek, the language of the New Testament: 'We have found the Messiah' (John 1:41) and 'He will baptise you with the Holy Spirit and with fire' (Matthew 3:11). With the divine child held by Our Lady, each of the three images of saints thus directs our attention to Christ. On either side of the Sanctuary are two large and ornate standard candlesticks, copies of sixteenth century originals in the Charterhouse of Pavia. They were given to Pluscarden by the Revd John Hardie Duthie, an Episcopalian Minister.

Against the south wall of the Sanctuary is the organ which is used to accompany Lauds, Vespers and Compline. On Sundays and Feast days, Mass and Benediction are also accompanied, and we usually have a small congregation who join in singing the chant ordinaries. The pipe organ is found to be very helpful in maintaining pitch and for giving a rhythmic lead when the whole community sings. Apart from this strictly functional role, the organ is also used for solo voluntaries, especially on more festive occasions. In the 1990s the community was dissatisfied with the current organ, built in the 1890s and the only known work of an amateur builder called James Graham from Carnoustie. Dr John Rowntree produced a specification for a new instrument which would cover the needs of the chant and also cater for a considerable repertoire of solo organ music. Kenneth Tickell of Northampton was then awarded the contract to build an instrument according to this specification which would blend with its surroundings and be a noble addition to the Sanctuary. The casework is of light oak. The organ is slim, only 1 metre deep, with panelling similar to that of the choirstalls. The pipe screen, designed by a member of the community, has a hexagonal design recalling the wild honey eaten by John the Baptist (Matthew 3:4) and fleurs-de-lys as a symbol of Our Lady. All the pipes are enclosed inside the swell-box, except for the Open Diapason (which forms the prospect) and the Subbass. For the sake of compactness, all of the enclosed 8' stops share the lowest octave, which belongs to the Stopped Diapason; and the two manuals share the same soundboard. The swell shutters are immediately behind the Open Diapason. The specification is as follows:

Kenneth Tickell's new organ in the choir

Manual 1		Manual 2		Pedal	
Open Diapason	8'	Clarabella	8'	Subbass	16'
Stopped Diapason	8'	Salicional	8'	Manual 1 to Pedal	
Principal	4'	Voix Céleste	8'	Manual 2 to Pedal	
Fifteenth	2'	Flute	4'		
Sesquialtera	II				

The organ was blessed for liturgical use in July 1998 and since then it has been a continuous source of delight. In September 1998 there was a public recital by Joseph Cullen as part of the community's Golden Jubilee celebrations. The Scottish composer James MacMillan composed an organ piece specially for the recital: 'Gaudeamus in Loci Pace'.

Behind the Altar one can see the Choir Stalls where the brethren sit at Mass and the Divine Office. They were given by a local family and constitute a fine example of contemporary church woodwork from the workshops of Robert Thompson, the famous 'mouse-man' of Kilburn in Yorkshire. Each stall has a 'misericord' on which the monk can lean while standing during the long choir-services and, in accordance with a mediaeval custom, many of these are carved by Dom Vincent Dapré, Marvin Elliott, Ian Lloyd-Osborne and Stephen Nemethy.

In the north wall above the Choir Stalls there is a finely-carved Sacrament House to hold the Reserved Sacrament, showing the figures of two kneeling angels holding a Monstrance.

A Monstrance is used in the service called Benediction to show to the faithful the consecrated bread of the Eucharist which Catholics believe is Christ himself, as he said,

'This is my body'.

This belief was repudiated by Protestants and in the decades before the Reformation a number of these Sacrament Houses were built in North East Scotland and decorated with similar designs to emphasise the local people's belief in the presence of Christ in the Sacrament. Today the Pluscarden Sacrament House is used to hold the Holy Oils and the Blessed Sacrament is reserved on the Lady Chapel Altar. On the south wall, partly obscured by wooden cupboards, are three comparatively well-preserved medieval stone *sedilia*, the seats for the Priest and ministers at Mass; the modern chairs used for this purpose are against the west wall of the sanctuary. Below the windows are more consecration crosses.

Architecturally this part of the Abbey presents several teasing problems, not the least interesting of which is the correspondence between the mason's marks found on the stones here and those at Hexham Abbey in Northumberland. All about the walls there are signs of altered planning and rebuilding that have produced unexpected contradictions in the symmetry of mouldings and window-openings. Originally the Choir, like the Crossing under the Tower, was vaulted in stone and evidence of this can be seen high up on the walls. Vaulting in the Transept Aisles was common at the time, but stone vaulting in the main spaces was rare and a sign of great distinction in the thirteenth century. In a document of 1457 it was said that the vaults of the Choir and crossing were in danger of collapse. The wall at the west end of the Choir is a later, probably fifteenth century, insert; the Valliscaulian choir stalls would have extended under the tower and perhaps even partly down the Nave.

The Choir windows were originally much larger than they are now. The view of the East Window from outside shows that it was originally a vast wall of glass which was later largely filled in with stone, possibly after the damage suffered in the fourteenth century. A similar infilling was done to the West window of Sweetheart Abbey after a fire there in 1397. In the thirteenth century the Choir would have been filled with light but it must have been terribly cold in a Scottish midwinter. Stumps of the original bar tracery included in the filling of the side windows are related to tracery first used at Glasgow and Elgin Cathedrals in the 1260s or 1270s and thus the Choir is unlikely to have been completed before this time. The beauty of the design can be seen in the 'spherical triangle' or trinity window high up above the transept chapels on the south side of the choir; the same shape is found at Valliscaulian Beauly. In its original conception, in fact, the windows of Pluscarden Choir must have made it a medieval wonder, and even today the east gable wall, with its four lancets, triplelight, aureole and trefoil openings topping each other, fires the imagination.

On the north side of the Choir is a door which gives access to the Dunbar Vestry. Curiously, a sepulchral slab has been used as the lintel of the communicating door to the Church and this memorial stone, conceivably of the 13th century, may well be the oldest monument surviving in

the Abbey today. From the outside of the Church, the Vestry can be seen as a curiously placed addition that nestles between the Choir and the North Transept. It is a late construction and was probably built by the last pre-Reformation Prior, Alexander Dunbar: the Dunbar arms with a crozier behind appear upon the roof-boss. A stair within the wall gives access to the room above which was probably used as a treasury, as was the case with the earlier sacristy at the Abbey of Arbroath. The Dunbar Vestry was restored in 1987 and is now used as the Sacristy.

The Dunbar Arms on the roof-boss in the Dunbar Vestry

It may also be of interest to mention before quitting the choir that in the 17th century it was termed the *Ogilvie Aisle* and served as a burying place for the Ogilvie family who lived nearby, some of whose tombstones can still be seen in the Transepts.

STAINED GLASS AT PLUSCARDEN

WHY HAVE HOLY IMAGES ?

'The Word became flesh and lived among us', John 1:14). These words from the beginning of St John's Gospel teach us that Jesus Christ is both truly a man and truly God. This mystery, which we call the Incarnation and celebrate at Christmas, is a turning point in human history and reveals the purpose and dignity of the whole material creation. All the glories of Christian figurative art depend on this doctrine. Before this mystery was accomplished in the womb of Mary, it was impossible to make a picture of the invisible God; now, because God has become man in Jesus, he can be depicted. Therefore to reject holy images is to deny that Jesus has come in the flesh and thus implicitly to deny our salvation.

HISTORY

All Pluscarden's medieval glass has been lost except a few fragments, some of which are in the display case by the West door of the Church. From these it seems that at least some of the medieval windows had *grisaille* glass. This, as in the famous 'Five Sisters' window at York Minster, involved plain glass, pale green in the Pluscarden fragments, with a painted foliate design and sometimes medallions of colour: one of the fragments was coloured pale blue. As the building is being restored the windows are being filled with striking modern designs, mostly made by monks in the Abbey's stained glass workshop. The community began the making of windows

twentieth century and the craft was continued when they moved to Prinknash. After the first monks came to Pluscarden in 1948 a stained glass workshop was established here and work by the monks can be found all over Scotland and even further afield. Dom Ninian Sloane and Br Gilbert Taylor were the main craftsmen involved.

The creation of stained glass windows for Churches is an art over a thousand years old. Traditionally coloured glass is cut to shape and joined by lead strips. This is the main technique used at Pluscarden, but a new technique developed in the last century is the thick slab glass know as *dalles de verre*, literally 'glass paving slabs'. In this method the slab of glass is cut, faceted and set in a matrix: epoxy resin in Br. Gilbert's windows, concrete in Sadie's. The Peter Shiach window also contains a technical innovation: paintwork fired into the glass, highly unusual in slab-glass windows. In direct sunlight *dalles de verre* gives a jewel-like sparkling which is seen at its best in the window high up in the south wall of the South Transept.

THE PLUSCARDEN WINDOWS:

THE CHOIR

THE EAST WINDOW OF THE CHOIR:
CHRIST OUR EUCHARIST
Br Gilbert (1983) leaded glass.
The names of the donors are on the glass.

As a backdrop to the High Altar, this window has a Eucharistic theme, from the wheat and grapes in the lower panes to Christ himself, holding his body and blood under the forms of bread and wine in the upper window. It can perhaps best be understood through the symbolism of the colours. The four lower pointed lancets represent creation, our world with its 'four corners'; red (blood) suggests humanity and animal life while the greens and browns suggest vegetative and inanimate creation. The grapes and wheat, fruit of the earth and warmed by the golden sun, are made into the bread and wine of the Mass. The created world, like the four lancets, points up to the Risen Christ, the Lord of Creation, shown as both God (white) and man (red). He is in Heaven (blue) and holds the bread and wine of the Eucharist, which has been transformed into his Body and Blood to give life to the world. The red in the top window shows that,

in Christ, man enters heaven to be transfigured and deified, a process of which Baptism is the beginning and the Eucharist the means. St Athanasius teaches that in Christ, 'God became man so that men might become gods'; and for St Paul, 'creation itself will be set free from its bondage to decay and obtain the glorious liberty of the children of God' (Romans 8:21). Thus as well as being a carpet of colour for the austere stone of the monastic Choir this window teaches the central truth of the Christian Faith.

THE TRANSEPT CHAPELS

THE VISITATION : NORTH TRANSEPT CHAPEL.
Br Gilbert (1965) leaded glass. A gift in memory of Elizabeth Muir of California.

The Gospel of Luke (1:39-56) tells us that when Mary accepted the Angel's message that she was to be Mother of God she ran to share the news with her relative Elizabeth, who was also with child. The striking composition of the figures in this window is based on a design traditional in the middle ages. It captures the joy of their meeting and is remarkable for showing the two babies in the womb, Jesus (on the left) and John the Baptist, who leapt for joy when Mary arrived. Mary's response was her great song of praise, the Magnificat, which is sung every day at the evening service of Vespers.

SYMBOLS OF THE FOUR EVANGELISTS AND AGNUS DEI : NORTH TRANSEPT CHAPEL
Br Gilbert (1985) leaded glass.

The gift of the Grant family. It makes use of Gloucester reamy glass to admit light into a dark corner, and selenium glass to give brightness and colour to the centre.

OUR LADY AND CHILD : IN THE INTERIOR WALL OF THE NORTH TRANSEPT CHAPEL
Br Gilbert, leaded glass. Originally exhibited at the Glasgow Vocations Exhibition 1960.

WINDOW IN THE EAST WALL OF THE SOUTH TRANSEPT CHAPEL
Br Gilbert (1998) leaded glass.

This window is dedicated to the daughters of John Slevin's family, all named Mary, so Marian symbols predominate.

THE TRANSEPTS

MARIAN WINDOW: NORTH WALL OF THE NORTH TRANSEPT
Sadie McLellan (1964-67) dalles de verre.

This window, donated by Neil and Philippa Petrie, celebrates the place of the Blessed Virgin Mary in the history of Salvation. The roundel is based on chapter 12 of the Book of Revelation and symbolises the universe divided between the darkness of the dragon and the Light of Christ, shining through the Woman (Mary-the Church). The inner circle is the earth, under the power of Satan, but from it come wheat and grapes which will become the Body and Blood of Christ, shown here as a child, who will defeat the dragon on the cross. This is the cosmic battle between good and evil and each one of us must choose on which side he or she stands. The seven doves of the central panel are the seven gifts of the Holy Spirit and the rest of the window shows the Rosary and various titles of Mary : *Middle left: The House of Gold* as the Divine Dwelling Place; *The Lily* for Chastity; *The Mirror* to reflect Christ; *The Enclosed Garden* for Virginity. *Middle centre: The Seven Gifts of the Holy Spirit* (Isaiah 11.2). *Middle right: The Star* to herald Christ; *The Rose of Sharon; The Gate of Heaven. Lower left: The Crown of Mary* and *The Rosary. Lower centre: The Lily among the Thorns* for Mary the sinless. *Lower right: The Star* that leads to Christ.

SS Benedict and Gregory: West Wall of the North Transept
Br Gilbert (1988) dalles de verre. The gift of James Boyle.

Against the red background of this window, St Benedict holds his Rule and below him stands his symbol the raven, St Gregory tells us that one brought him bread when he was living as a hermit as a young man. Pope St Gregory the Great (c540-604) is a Doctor (teacher) of the Church and wrote the Life of St Benedict. He sent monks to convert the English to Christianity and also played an important part in the development of Latin Church Music. This is called Gregorian Chant after him, and is sung here at Pluscarden. The dove by his ear illustrates the legend that the melodies of the chant were dictated to him by the Holy Spirit.

SS Peter, Patrick, Margaret and Celtic Saints with Pluscarden Abbey: West Wall of the North Transept
Br Gilbert (1992) dalles de verre. Given in memory Peter Shiach.

It emphasises that the ancient Church of Celtic Scotland was always in communion with the Pope, the successor of St Peter.

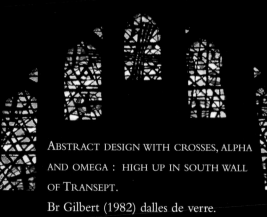

Abstract design with crosses, alpha and omega : high up in south wall of Transept.
Br Gilbert (1982) dalles de verre.

creation itself will be set free from its bondage to dec

THE LADY CHAPEL

THE CITY OF GOD AND THE MONK'S JOURNEY

Centre and right lights, Dom Ninian (1958-60); left light Br Gilbert (1960). leaded glass.

In memory of Alexander Bonnyman who came from a local family but died in Tennessee. The right light shows a man coming from the world to enter the monastery, ending with his Solemn Profession; the left light continues the monk's life to his death, showing, by the words ORA ET LABORA (prayer and work), monks working, praying and tempted by the devil.

ST ANDREW

Crear McCartney (c1957) leaded glass.

STAINED GLASS IN OTHER PARTS OF THE MONASTERY

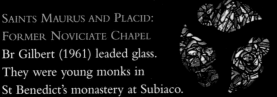

SAINTS MAURUS AND PLACID: FORMER NOVICIATE CHAPEL

Br Gilbert (1961) leaded glass. They were young monks in St Benedict's monastery at Subiaco. St Gregory tells us that on one occasion Placid fell into the lake and Benedict told Maurus to fetch him out. He did this not realising that he was running on the water and so by his obedience miraculously saved his brother from drowning. The scene is dramatically captured in this roundel.

CRUCIFIX WITH OUR LADY AND ST JOHN : REFECTORY

Dom Ninian (1957) leaded glass.

KING SOLOMON ON HIS THRONE : SLYPE LIBRARY

Eddie Ryan (c1959) leaded glass
This window depicts the great ivory throne of Solomon described in 1 Kings 10:18-20.

THE CLOISTER

While the visitor enjoys the privilege of seeing the Abbey Church of Pluscarden and of walking in the precincts, there is much of the Abbey that he must respect as personal and private to the present-day community. It may help his appreciation of the Abbey as a whole, however, if we describe briefly the plan of the buildings that surround the Cloister. The Cloister itself is about 100 feet square and has a garden called the Cloister-garth at its centre.

The Lady Chapel

The carved panel of St Benedict in the Lady Chapel

Immediately south of the Transept Aisles, and observable through the squint, is the Lady Chapel which we have already mentioned. The Altar is dedicated in honour of the Nativity of Our Lady and the chapel was the first part of the Church used by the community when they returned in 1948. In the Chapel a group of memorial stones includes one of 1527 to Alexander Dunbar of Durris, one of the heritable baillies of Pluscarden, and a wall tablet to Mr Francis Hasben, 'late preacher of the Gospel here in Pluscarden' who died in 1777. A second Altar dedicated to St Benedict stands beyond the Chapel's wooden screen.

The restoration of the East Cloister walkway was completed in 1986. The apartments beyond the Lady Chapel, forming the east side of the cloisters, begin with the Chapter House, a beautiful room whose medieval vaulting is supported by a central column. Some medieval roof-bosses survive, one with a representation of the *Agnus Dei.*

East Cloister walkway

65

The library

The monks and guests taking lunch in the Refectory

The Green Man

South of the Cloisters are storehouses and workshops, but here stood originally the large Refectory of the Priory with kitchens extending in a long wing to the west and cellars to the east. Excavations in the 19th century and fragmentary remains suggest that the south range of the monastery was three stories high and that the undercroft and the refectory were vaulted and had a central line of columns. On this side the south cloister has been rebuilt and now contains part of the Abbey Library, but the site of the mediaeval Refectory awaits rebuilding. At the south-east corner, however, probably on the site of the Calefactory, a small Infirmary has been added with some cells above. The Calefactory of a medieval monastery was a room with a fire (*calefacere* in Latin means 'to make warm').

Next comes the Slype, a passage now forming part of the Library of the Abbey. It has a boss of a 'green man' in the vaulting. Then comes what in the middle ages was the Day Room, with its vault supported on two pillars, which has been divided to provide Refectory and kitchens. Above this wing are the dormitories, accessed from the Cloister by a narrow 'day-stair', with the small 'Prior's Chapel' at the north end which has a tiny sacristy attached and some traces of fresco on the walls.

On the West side of the cloister a new West Wing has been built, which was opened in 1994 and contains parlours and St Benedict's Guesthouse for male retreatants. The Appeal which raised the money to pay for this was the work of a number of friends of the Abbey. The drive has been extended round to its door and a fine garden has been laid out and planted in front of the West Range by John Clark for the use of the community and resident guests. Excavations on the site before building work began discovered that a substantial West Range was not part of the original 13th century plan, but a flimsy structure was erected against the West wall of the Cloister some time after the Priory was united with Urquhart.

*The guest table and
pulpit in the Refectory*

*Retreat at
Pluscarden*

*Courtesy of
Sacro Speco, Subiaco*

A similar development occurred at the Premonstratensian Abbey of Dryburgh in the Borders. In the Cistercian plan followed at Pluscarden, the West Range was for the lay brothers and it may be that either there were very few such brothers when Pluscarden was built or that with the Valliscaulians they were more closely integrated with the Choir monks.

Outside the enclosure wall, to the right of the main gate of the Abbey is St Scholastica's Retreat House, named after St Benedict's sister. This long, low building provides accommodation for female guests and was opened in 1990.

St Scholastica

St Scholastica's Retreat House

Souvenirs may be purchased at the Gift Shop. If the visitor is tempted, he will have the satisfaction of knowing that he has not only acquired a worthwhile token of a visit he is never likely to forget, but also that he has helped in a small way the life and work of this community who are dedicated to the worship of God and to the rehabilitation of this royal and ancient monastic house.

The West Range: St Benedict's Guesthouse and the main entrance

A Glance at Pluscarden History

 c.1070

St Margaret of Scotland founds a monastery at
Dunfermline with Benedictines from Canterbury.

c.1136

St David I, King of Scots, founds Urquhart Priory for
Benedictines from Dunfermline.

1150

St David I founds Kinloss Abbey by Findhorn Bay for
Cistercian monks from Melrose.

 1193

Blessed Viard founds the Priory of Val des Choux.

1203

Abbey of Iona refounded for Benedictine monks.

 1214-1249

Alexander II, King of Scots.

1228

A rising in Moray by the MacWilliams put down
by the Earl of Buchan.

VALLISCAULIAN PLUSCARDEN

1230

Three Valliscaulian monasteries established in Scotland:
King Alexander II founds Pluscarden Priory,
John Byset of Lovat founds Beauly Priory,
Duncan McDougall founds Ardchattan Priory on
Loch Etive.

1239

Simon, Prior of Pluscarden.

? John Frer, Prior of Pluscarden.

? John Suryass, Prior of Pluscarden.

1262

Bull of Pope Urban IV confirming and protecting the
privileges of Pluscarden.

1264

Andrew, Prior of Pluscarden, later Abbot of Kinloss.

1274

William, Prior of Pluscarden.

Bagimond's Tax Roll, Pluscarden assessed for £533
annual income.

1286

Simon, Prior of Pluscarden.

 1296

Edward I of England and his army at Elgin.

1303

Edward I of England in Moray, based at Kinloss Abbey.

1345

John Wise, Prior of Pluscarden.

1367-98

Thomas Fullonis, Prior of Pluscarden.

1390

The Wolf of Badenoch burns Forres and Elgin,
and probably Pluscarden.

1398

Alexander of Pluscarden, Prior of Pluscarden.

c.1417

Eoghann MacPheadair, Prior of Pluscarden. David Cran,
monk of Deer briefly intruded as Prior of Pluscarden.

1428

Andrew Symson, monk of Deer,
Prior of Pluscarden.

1435

Richard Lundy, monk of Melrose, provided as Prior of Pluscarden but did not take up the office. The monks of Pluscarden elect William Birnie, one of their number, as Prior, this was challenged by Symson and the law suit continued until 1439.

>1447

William Hagis, monk of Pluscarden, elected Prior of Pluscarden. Election disputed by William Birnie.

BENEDICTINE PLUSCARDEN I
1454

Union of Pluscarden with Urquhart, by the Papal Bull *Ad apicem*.

John Bonally, monk of Dunfermline and Prior of Urquhart, Prior of Pluscarden.

1456-1476

William Boyce, monk of Dunfermline, Prior of Pluscarden.

1461

The *Liber Pluscardensis* written at the Priory.

1476-1480

Thomas Foster, monk of Dunfermline, Prior of Pluscarden.

1479

Gavin Dunbar, cleric of Moray Diocese, attempts to become Prior of Pluscarden.

1481-1486?

David Boyce, monk of Arbroath, Prior of Pluscarden, although Robert Harrower, monk of Dunfermline, had been elected by the community.

1487-1509

Robert Harrower, Prior of Pluscarden.

1506

King James IV visits Pluscarden.

1509-1529

George Learmonth, cleric of St Andrews Archdiocese, Prior of Pluscarden, having become a monk.

1518

Gavin Dunbar, Dean of Moray, becomes Bishop of Aberdeen.

1529

George Learmonth, Prior of Pluscarden provided as coadjutor to Gavin Dunbar, Bishop of Aberdeen.

1529-1560

Alexander Dunbar, canon of Ross Diocese, Prior of Pluscarden, having become a monk.

1531

George Learmonth dies in March, a year before Bishop Gavin Dunbar.

1548

Three of Prior Alexander's sons legitimated.

1555

The 'Bloody Vespers' in Elgin Cathedral.

1560

August: Reformation Parliament.

19th September: death of Prior Alexander Dunbar.

COMMENDATORY PRIORS
1561

Master William Cranston, Prior of Pluscarden 1561-2.

George, 5th Lord Seton, *Yconomus* of Pluscarden.

1565-1595

Alexander Seton, Prior of Pluscarden.

1567

George Seton helps Mary, Queen of Scots, escape from Lochleven castle.

1571

Alexander Seton sent to the Jesuits in Rome for education.

1577

Alexander Seton deprived of Pluscarden for not conforming to Protestantism.

1577–82

James Douglas intruded as Prior of Pluscarden.

1587

Pluscarden erected into a temporal lordship, Alexander Seton becomes Lord Urquhart.

LAY PRIORS

1595–1611

Kenneth Mackenzie of Kintail, lay-Prior of Pluscarden.

1611–1633

Colin Mackenzie, 2nd Lord Kintail, lay-Prior of Pluscarden.

1633–1649

Thomas Mackenzie of Kintail, lay-Prior of Pluscarden.

1649–1655

Sir George Mackenzie of Tarbet, lay-Prior of Pluscarden.

1655–1662

Sir George Mackenzie, lay-Prior of Pluscarden.

1662–1664

George Sinclair, Earl of Caithness, and Major George Bateman lay-Priors of Pluscarden.

1664–1687

Major George Bateman, sole lay-Prior of Pluscarden.

1687–1709

James Grant, lay-Prior of Pluscarden.

Rood screen angel

1709-1763

William Duff of Dipple, later 1st Earl of
Fife, lay-Prior of Pluscarden.

1763-1809

James, 2nd Earl of Fife, lay-Prior of Pluscarden.

1809-1811

Alexander, 3rd Earl of Fife, lay-Prior of Pluscarden.

1811-1857

James, 4th Earl of Fife, lay-Prior of Pluscarden.

1857-1879

James, 5th Earl of Fife, lay-Prior of Pluscarden.

1879-1889

Alexander, 6th Earl & 1st Duke of Fife,
lay-Prior of Pluscarden.

1889-1900

John Patrick, 3rd Marquess of Bute, lay-
Prior of Pluscarden.

1896

*Aelred Carlyle founds an Anglican
Benedictine community.*

1900-1945

Lord Colum Crichton-Stuart, lay-Prior
of Pluscarden.

1913

*Abbot Aelred Carlyle and the monks of Caldey received
into the Catholic Church.*

1928

The monks of Caldey move to Prinknash

Map of Caldey Island

BENEDICTINE PLUSCARDEN II

1945-1948

Dom Benedict Steuart, titular Prior of Pluscarden.

1948

Monastic Observance re-established at Pluscarden.

1948-1951

Dom Brendan McHugh

(Local Superior and acting Prior).

1950

Dom Wilfred Upson, Abbot of Prinknash (1938-
1963) declared *de jure* Prior of Pluscarden by the
Lord Lyon, King of Arms.

1951-1961

Dom Norbert Cowin (Local Superior and acting Prior).

1963

Dom Dyfrig Rushton, Abbot of Prinknash (1963-
1979) and Major Superior of Pluscarden (1963-66)

1961-1966

Dom Columba Wynne

(Local Superior and acting Prior).

1966

Pluscarden becomes an independent conventual Priory.

1966-1974

Dom Alfred Spencer,
Conventual Prior.

1974

Pluscarden becomes an Abbey.

1974-1992

Rt Rev Dom Alfred Spencer, 1st Abbot of Pluscarden.

1992-

Rt Rev Dom Hugh Gilbert,
2nd Abbot of Pluscarden.

AFTERWORD

'Who went quickly among the trees
Disturbing that blackbird?'
Finnbar stopped here at sunset
Finnbar from Pluscarden
Going on to Walsingham, Compostela.
We put bandages on his feet,
A crust in his bowl.

Finnbar has sat so long
In the scriptorium
How will his white feet endure
The Pyrenees and the Alps?

From *Foresterhill*
by George Mackay Brown.

Poems on pages 21 and 76